JAZZ GUITAR
FRETBOARD NAVIGATION

From *Bach* to **BEBOP**

MARK WHITE

To access video visit:
www.halleonard.com/mylibrary

Enter Code
8408-8181-0295-0910

*For Barbara M. White, a very powerful talent and
dedicated musician, who started all the music for me.*

BERKLEE PRESS

Editor in Chief: Jonathan Feist
Senior Vice President of Online Learning and Continuing Education/CEO of Berklee Online: Debbie Cavalier
Assistant Vice President of Marketing and Recruitment for Berklee Online: Mike King
Dean of Continuing Education: Carin Nuernberg
Editorial Assistants: Emily Jones, Eloise Kelsey
Cover Design: Mammoth Design
Cover and Author Photos: Jonathan Feist

RECORDING

Bass: John Pierce
Drums: John Hazilla
Guitar: Mark White
Bill Brinkley (Guitar II parts on the Bach pieces)
Keyboards: Scott deOgburn

Engineer: Mark White, Gorgon Studio

ISBN 978-0-87639-172-3

Berklee
Press

1140 Boylston Street
Boston, MA 02215-3693 USA
(617) 747-2146

Visit Berklee Press Online at
www.berkleepress.com

Berklee Online

online.berklee.edu

DISTRIBUTED BY

HAL•LEONARD®
CORPORATION
7777 W. BLUEMOUND RD. P.O. BOX 13819
MILWAUKEE, WISCONSIN 53213

Visit Hal Leonard Online
www.halleonard.com

Berklee Press, a publishing activity of Berklee College of Music, is a not-for-profit educational publisher.
Available proceeds from the sales of our products are contributed to the scholarship funds of the college.

CONTENTS

ACKNOWLEDGMENTS

Many people contributed to the making of this book. I'd like to give thanks to Susanna Chivian for proofing the initial drafts; to Jonathan Feist, editor in chief of Berklee Press, for the opportunity to do this project and for patience, wisdom, and good-sense guidance through the entire process, without ever being heavy-handed; to Larry Baione, chair of the Berklee Guitar department, for encouragement and backing the project; to Kim Perlak for guidance on Baroque performance practices; to Tony Germain, Stephanie Tiernan, and Bob Winter for information regarding Bach and *The Well-Tempered Clavier*; to Bill Brinkley for help preparing some of the initial Finale scores and playing on the recordings; to Emily Jones and Eloise Kelsey at Berklee Press for the extremely time consuming and challenging job of transferring my handwritten manuscripts to Finale files and tablature; to all the musicians involved in recording the audio: John Pierce (bass), John Hazilla (drums), Scott de Ogburn (keyboards), and Bill Brinkley (guitar II parts on the Bach pieces); to Peter Kontrimas for support, feedback, and ears regarding the recording; to Bryant Trenier of Trenier Guitars, Howard Paul and Bob Benedetto of Benedetto Guitars; to Jimmy D'Aquisto and John Buscarino for their marvelous guitars and amps all used in the recording of the audio; to Craig and A.J. Jones of Bay State Vintage Guitars for studio gear and amp maintenance; to Antonio Mendoza for invaluable insight regarding this project and guitar playing in general; to several excellent Berklee guitarists for proofreading the jazz pieces: Jonathan Richer, Eric Palmer, Nick Reczek, Ben Bass, Billy Wilkins, Rodrigo Gramitto, and Jan Vincent Huntenburg; to all my amazing teachers; and especially, to all my terrific students from all over the world, past and present, for their persistent encouragement, inspiring abilities, and loyalty. It's been a great pleasure to learn and work with all of you! I take great pride in your achievements.

INTRODUCTION

This book is about linear fretboard navigation on the guitar. The word "linear" implies line, and the jazz pieces in this book are linear jazz solos. The Bach pieces are mostly comprised of two lines (parts), and sometimes, as many as four lines.

"Linear" doesn't mean that there isn't any harmony in the pieces. Far from it! And while there are some voiced chords here and there, harmony abounds in all these pieces. It's linear harmony. The Boppers used to have a saying: "The line is the chord, and the chord is the line." Pearls of wisdom!

I became acquainted with the Bach pieces, included here, as a kid. My mother, an accomplished pianist, had a daily practice routine that included Chopin and Bach repertoire, among others, but especially Bach pieces from *The Well-Tempered Clavier*. She was trained by Elizabeth Zug, an excellent pianist, who was much lauded for her performances at Town Hall in NYC, among others. Elizabeth Zug's teacher had been Alberto Jonás, a Spanish born virtuoso and noted piano pedagogue. Jonas had been a student of the famous virtuoso pianist and pedagogue, Anton Rubinstein, one of the most celebrated pianists of all time.

Pianists are often associated with "schools" of piano playing. These schools tend to revolve around celebrated pianists or treatises on technique, like the Whiteside or "English School," or the "Russian School" (Rubenstein, etc.). Along with the "schools" are to be found many different editions of the great composers' works, edited by (in the case of piano music) some of musical history's great pianists and piano pedagogues. The edition I used for reference here is by Hans Bischoff, a nineteenth-century German concert pianist and pedagogue who studied with Theodor Kullak, who was a student of Carl Czerny, who was taught by Beethoven! This is the edition my mother used. The manuscript has been heavily annotated by Elizabeth Zug.

"Schools of jazz guitarists" reference great players, like Charlie Christian or Wes Montgomery and the other guitarists they influenced, in a family-tree kind of lineage. This is more stylistic conception than specific, technical, how-to-play-it information. Offshoots of the Charlie Christian "school," like Barney Kessel and Herb Ellis, were frequently described as "disciples" of Charlie Christian. And while Barney did a really cool, swingin' album based on Bizet's *Carmen* and was an early pioneer of jazz guitar education, not too many jazz guitarists outside of Barry Galbraith have done large-scale recorded Bach projects.

Jazz guitar educators work within schools, especially colleges. Bill Leavitt, a longtime chair of Berklee's guitar department, adapted a large body of traditional classical guitar pieces (which included several of Bach's two-part inventions) arranged for pick-style guitar. These, along with his magnum opus *A Modern Method for Guitar*, helped further many great guitarists' careers. These pieces were widely used as performance, reading, and even as ensemble materials within Berklee's guitar department curriculum.

Some of Bill's students at Berklee, such as Mick Goodrick, John Abercrombie, John Scofield, Mike Stern, and others (including a very young adjunct professor, named Pat Metheny) were sometimes referred to informally as "The Boston School of Guitar Playing." Berklee has turned out more "star" guitarist alumni than any other institution on this or any other planet!

I've been playing Bach for over forty years, on and off. I started playing *The Well-Tempered Clavier* pieces *again* a couple of years back with a fellow guitarist and colleague, Bill Brinkley. As I learned the pieces, it dawned on me how similar the organization of content and playing the Bach and preparing/playing jazz solo transcriptions were. I know from experience as a jazz educator and guitarist how difficult it can be to organize challenging musical content into logical fingering locations on the fingerboard. Furthermore, the organizational concept has to facilitate the technical rendering of the pieces, while achieving excellent "musical" results, both for phrasing and "flow." And that was the beginning of how this book came about.

How to Use This Book

This book explores some organizational concepts (discussed in part I) to consider in performing the pieces. The greatest benefit will come from learning and playing the pieces in part II. All the jazz "etudes" are fingered completely, beginning to end. The Bach pieces have the top part fingered with the exception of the beginning piece, the C major fugue, which has the first two parts fingered. The second parts are deliberately left unfingered and without tablature, for you to complete. Use this as a workbook, and write in your fingerings! All the music has included guitar tab to assist those who don't read standard music notation (primarily) as a means of learning music. Again, the second tab parts are left blank for you to complete, if you prefer this medium.

The book's pieces, both jazz and Bach, are intended for "pick-style" guitar playing, and that's how I performed them on the accompanying recordings. It isn't a "deal breaker," by any means, if you don't play pick-style. Fingerstyle, played with thumb, and even tapping styles can be employed here, because the emphasis is on organizing the fingering hand.

The pieces are presented in pairs, mostly organized by key, as well as by similarities in harmonic language and fingering issues. The jazz pieces are based on standard jazz progressions from classic jazz tunes. I'm sure you'll see the similarity in approach for navigating/organizing all the pieces in both genres on the guitar fingerboard.

Each piece includes an audio demonstration track featuring all parts, plus one or more play-along tracks that are minus the lead line in the jazz pieces or each of the parts in the Bach.

 To access the accompanying audio, go to www.halleonard.com/mylibrary, and enter the code found on the first page of this book. This will grant you instant access to every example. Examples with accompanying audio are marked with an audio icon.

About the Bach Performances

Because of the narrower range of the guitar compared to piano, some compromises have been necessarily incorporated in arranging the Bach pieces for two guitars. Some of the pieces, namely the C major fugue and the C minor prelude, fit pretty comfortably on the guitar when transposed up an octave from the written keyboard register. In reality, because of the transposing factor on the guitar (sounding an octave lower than written), the music would sound in the same register as written on the piano anyway. The other pieces were originally written in registers that would sound "spindly" and are too difficult to play up an octave on guitar. "Octave compression" and "octave ducking" have been employed to make them playable. In a few places, the lines cross over each other briefly, but without using drop tunings, baritone tuning, or the like, there really wasn't a way around this. And the arrangements really sound good, so I don't think JSB would mind!

General observation: Much of the Bach used here is written in sixteenth notes vs. the jazz pieces where most of the lines are in eighth notes (though "Tsunami Mommy" has quite a few double-time sixteenth lines starting in the middle). The Bach pieces are generally slower in tempo and the jazz pieces are faster in these selections, which explains the choice of sixteenths vs. eighths. Typically, slower-tempo jazz ballads, funk, and rock tunes tend to contain more "double-time" lines in sixteenth notes. Up-tempo jazz tunes tend to be oriented toward eighth notes as the primary rhythmic unit. It varies drastically, but it's all about time!

Over the years, there have been many editions of books and recordings for electric guitar playing Bach, mostly as a kind of novelty sales point—complete with JSB sporting an electric guitar and sunglasses on the cover art. There have also been some performers playing "swinging" jazz renditions of Bach. I'm not making any judgment calls here, but the jazz pieces in this book are definitely meant to swing, the bossa/Latin will be more even eighth and sixteenth, and the Bach is just really fun and challenging to play on electric, acoustic, or any other kind of string instrument! They don't swing, but they certainly have their own groove!

In a lot of ways, J.S. Bach *was* really one of the first *jazz musicians*, in spirit—a brilliant keyboard virtuoso, improviser, a working musician, and teacher, all the while managing his life and family, while creating monumental art on a day after day basis. Some three hundred years later, there's still a lot to learn and enjoy from the man whose music travels the cosmos aboard NASA spacecraft. (Imagine being the first alien to hit the Play button!) Had he been born in our time, I like to think he'd be right at home in New York City, and jazz would be a passion for him. He just wouldn't have to take the harpsichords by horse-drawn carts to the coffee house gig on Friday nights!

It is my most sincere hope this book will help bring you closer to fulfillment on your musical journey!

~Mark White

PART I

Linear Fingering Concepts

1. MOVEABLE SCALE FORMS

The concept of movable scale grids has been around for a long time. The "CAGED" system and the Berklee system have been utilized by countless guitarists.

- The "CAGED" system was an early major scale organizer that Joe Pass showed me based on simple, open-string chord forms. Adding a barre with the first finger, the shapes become moveable. When each chord shape is transposed to the same key, the chord shapes formed a gridwork over the entire fingerboard for organizing musical content in any register.
- Berklee used an overlapping, similar method, designating the basic fingerings as type 1, 1A, 2, 3, and 4.

These two-octave scale grids cover the neck from low to high, cover all keys, can be used as master forms to derive other scale fingerings (like the modes of the major scale, other seven-tone scale varieties, etc.), and contain chord arpeggios and chord shapes (grips) related to the scale within the scale fingering.

When reading music and/or trying to organize notes on the guitar fingerboard, many guitarists get stuck in key-oriented scale fingerings. Sometimes, thinking by key can be a great organizational idea, such as when playing a blues-scale improv by key over a blues progression, for instance. But when dealing with music that contains more harmonically vertical content, the key/scale orientation often causes limitations that can compromise the phrasing, feel, and musicality of the material.

Here's an in-position E♭ major-scale fingering:

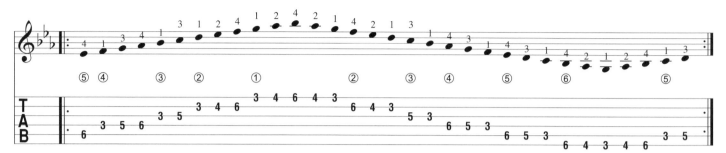

FIG. 1.1. In-Position E♭ Major-Scale Fingering

If you're playing a small melodic idea, such as in figures 1.2 and 1.3, it's fine to use a scale-derived fingering.

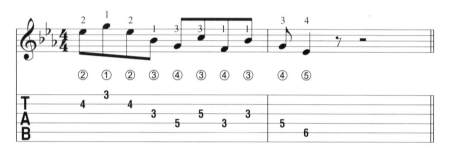

FIG. 1.2. Melody 1, Suitable for Scale-Derived Fingering

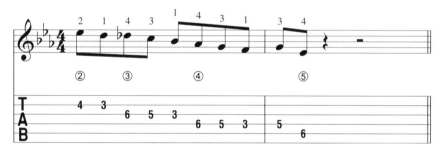

FIG. 1.3. Melody 2, Suitable for Scale-Derived Fingering

However, when playing longer lines with more diverse content, a strictly scale/key fingering becomes musically limiting and awkward—especially the old "finger stretches" utilized to stay "in the box." Ouch!

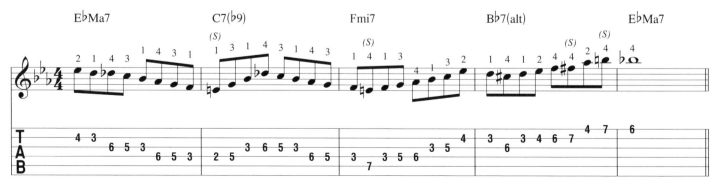

FIG. 1.4. Longer Line, In Position, Requiring Stretches

Figure 1.5 shows a refingering of the previous example. The phrasing and feel of the line improve dramatically by breaking down and identifying the musical components, then finding new fingering locations based on the individual elements of scale or chord shapes (arpeggios) on the fingerboard. The chromatics employed here either fit into the scale as in the first bar, or laterally approach chord tones on the same string (more about this later). Generally speaking, identifying the components makes this line easier to see on the fingerboard, and the added movement makes the phrasing more "musical" and more fun to play! Break out of the box!

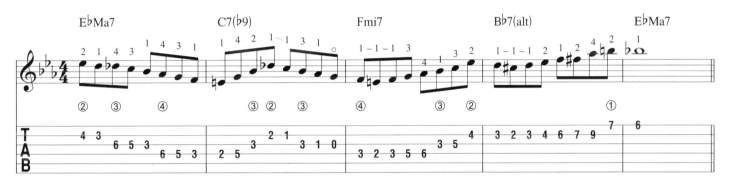

FIG. 1.5. Refingering for Greater Musicality

The "thinking" used in choosing fingerings for figure 1.5 would yield an analysis like this.

FIG. 1.6. Melodic/Fingering Analysis

So just to clarify, instead of playing all the content in a large E♭ major scale form because the key center is E♭ major, the individual scales and chord outlines that make up the line are used to derive the fingerings. This thinking is still related to the "in-position" scales and their related harmonic content. In fact, there's a whole network of in-position two-octave scales representing all the scales that relate to the chord progression in this area of activity. We're just using smaller, sometimes one-octave scales, arpeggios, chord shapes, and even just fragments of these components found within the bigger two-octave versions while following the individual chords that make up the progressions contained in these pieces.

I call this concept "smart boxes." The focus is on smaller parcels of musical information that move from one to another constantly, instead of staying "in the box." Employing more movement, especially laterally, yields a more horn-like or "breath-driven" quality on the guitar. Looking at any musical content this way leads to better phrasing, musicality, and a more "vertical" (harmonic) approach to fingerboard navigation.

2. FINGER SHIFTS

You'll have noticed in figure 1.5 multiple usages of finger shifts with the same finger. This is another game-changing concept that ties into the "smart box" idea. Finger shifts help link "smart boxes" together as one moves into another, like this:

FIG. 2.1. Finger Shifts Linking Triadic "Smart Boxes"

Playing a line like this in position would really kill the natural guitar instinct to move the shape down/up the same string group. The finger shifts help enable the connectivity. Finger shifts are also often utilized when adding chromatic approaches to outlines.

Here's another example of performing multiple finger shifts in the same line. Note the target notes (chord tones) and chromatics are always on the same string.

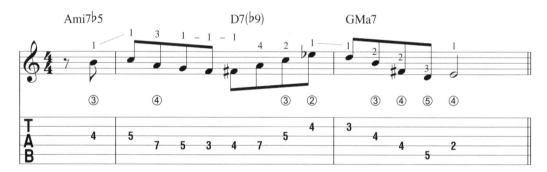

FIG. 2.2. Multiple Finger Shifts within a Line

3. SAME FINGER ON SAME FRET, ADJACENT STRINGS

While it seems an obvious choice in scale fingerings, using the same finger on the same fret, while moving laterally on adjacent strings, is new to some. I personally use this technique widely, and you'll find it frequently in the fingerings for the coming pieces. I was initially exposed to this concept in Bill Leavitt's *A Modern Method for Guitar* series of books (Berklee Press). Here's a typical fingering for a two-octave triad arpeggio using the same finger across adjacent strings where needed, "rolling" the finger, as Bill Leavitt described it, to obtain a more legato sound:

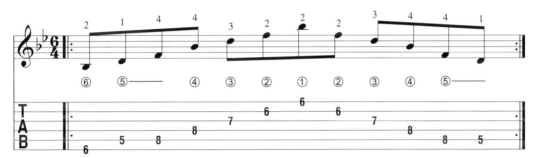

FIG. 3.1. "Rolling" Between Strings

Ultimately, smart boxes, finger shifts, using the same finger on adjacent strings, and other tactics all become incorporated in how we organize and execute content on the guitar fingerboard. But, classical and jazz lines can be elusive when it comes to mapping location and phrasing. One particularly strong unifying factor is playing or orienting into a chord shape, and many times these will necessitate using the "rolling" technique on adjacent strings, same fret. My studies with Joe Pass instilled in me a direct relationship between chord forms (grips) and lines that were derived from chord shapes. Joe could make the content of an improvised line flow from the chord shapes in a progression, like this turnaround.

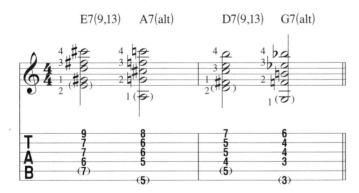

FIG. 3.2. Turnaround Chord Progression

Here is a characteristic line that Joe might have played over these chords:

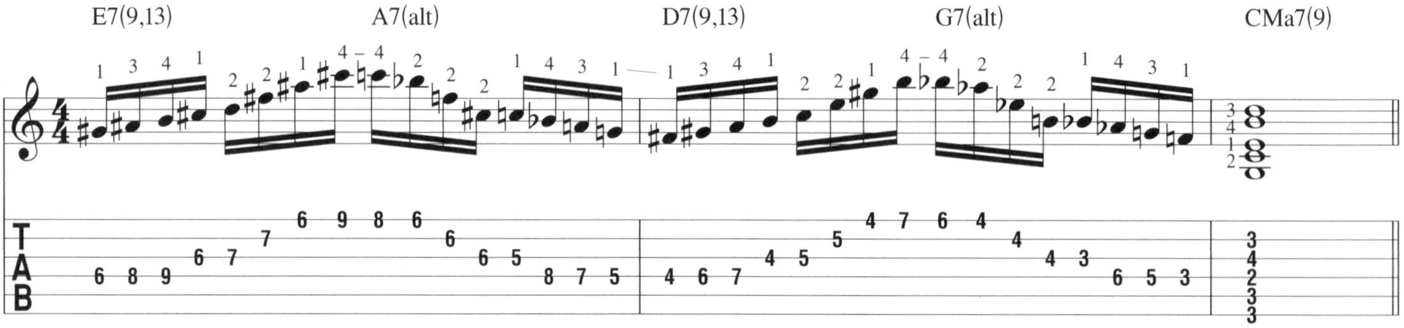

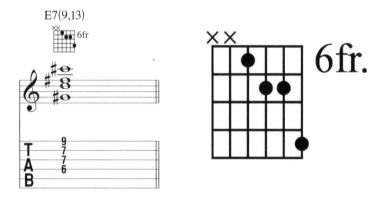

FIG. 3.3. Melodic Line Derived from Chords in Figure 3.2

You can see that using the same finger on adjacent strings, even in small amounts, facilitates playing the line. The line fingerings are slightly different from the chord grips in figure 3.2 in that they don't include the low note in parenthesis, which in these examples happen to be the roots. They also contain some passing notes from the scales these chords could be related to, like Lydian ♭7 on the (9,13) chords and altered on the 7(alt), so there's always the scale component in there too.

FIG. 3.4. Fingering Shape

This is the shape that generates the line in figure 3.3. It's a typical "smart shape" moving chromatically on the top set of strings. The shape is "inside" all the chords in figure 3.2. See it?

The "trick" to playing adjacent strings on the same fret is making the "rolled" notes sound balanced and not overly sustained compared to the rest of the notes in the line. Separate and slightly detach the adjacent notes until the line becomes uniform—like a scalar line. At that point, you can add inflections and articulation to make the music "speak." Here's another example, to clarify.

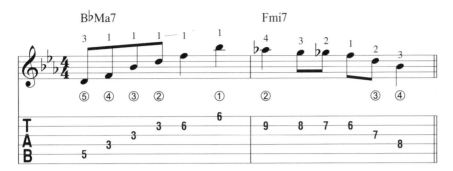

Fig. 3.5. Rolling Notes on Adjacent Strings

Adjacent string finger "rolling" is a really useful technique that uncomplicates while adding fluidity to fingerings. But, there are still times when you want to use *more* than one finger on the same fret, usually when you want the notes to ring into each other. The intro to "Soul Man" comes to mind with its parallel major sixth intervals. This would be played as a constant structure with the first finger on the G string and second finger on the high E string.

4. NON-SEQUENTIAL FINGERINGS AND OTHER ORIENTATIONS

Initially, many guitarists try to finger linear ideas sequentially—that is, one finger after another, one finger per fret. And of course, you can skip a finger where there's no note relating to a finger. In reality, while scale sequences (and for that matter, lots of other musical content) can work great this way, it's "seeing" the individual musical ideas that dictate location and how they might be fingered. If that wasn't complicated enough, there's the duplication of notes and multiple location choices for fingering on the guitar! So get ready for some new connectivity scenarios!

Here are some more ideas and the reasoning behind some of the fingerings used in this book.

Sequential Fingerings Across Strings

A fingering can be sequential, but can shift the finger sequence to another string even on the same fret. In the following example, it's two small melodic ideas that share the same scale. Finger 1 continues to finger 2, but on another string.

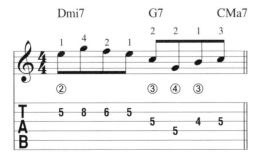

Fig. 4.1. Sequential Fingerings Across Strings

Lateral Scale Fingerings

Groupings of notes can follow a lateral scale fingering organized on the same string. Notice that the groupings ascend and then descend with the scale fragment on the G string (notes shown in parentheses).

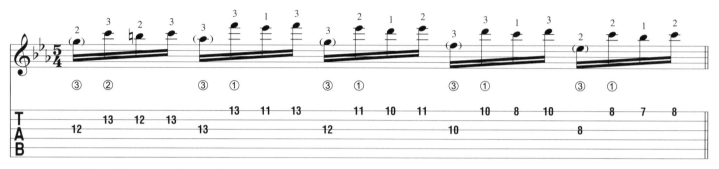

FIG. 4.2. Lateral Scale Fingering

Interval-Based Fingerings

Interval-based fingerings have been widely used for organizing all kinds of guitar music—especially the major second. This is a very strong "shape" that works all over the fingerboard. Check out Andrés Segovia's *Diatonic Major and Minor Scales*, for instance. Segovia often uses major second fingering 1,3–1,3 to shift upwards (and less frequently descending) on the same string through his scale fingerings. (There are some finger shifts in there too!)

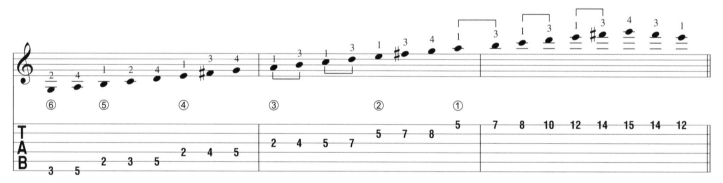

FIG. 4.3. Interval-Based Fingerings

Contemporary jazz guitar improv language utilizes interval shapes, too. Note that the major second can have a chromatic in between the outer notes and also this combination along with a "helper" note, turning the idea into a four-note grouping as found in the second bar, beats 3 and 4.

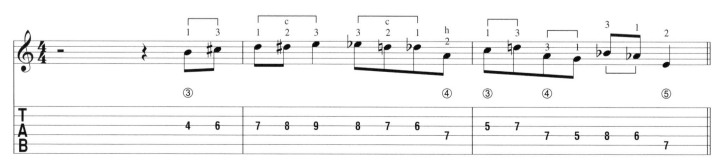

FIG. 4.4. Chromatics

Any interval shape like minor seconds, minor thirds, major thirds, fourths, etc. used in a recognizable pattern (chromatic, diatonic sequences, etc.) can be a good tool for organizing fingerings. They can be played across, diagonally, and laterally on the fingerboard. Larger intervals, such as fifths, sixths, sevenths, and compound intervals (ninths, tenths, etc.) use up more real estate, so to speak, and tend to be played more laterally.

Finger-to-Fret Orientation

Triads and triad arpeggios (close and spread, as well as all types), as seen in figure 2.1, follow a finger to a fret rationale. Parallel triads can move up or down the same string group. Notice that while moving step-wise or by a leap, the arpeggiated triad fingering, regardless of inversion, will relate back to the chord fingering.

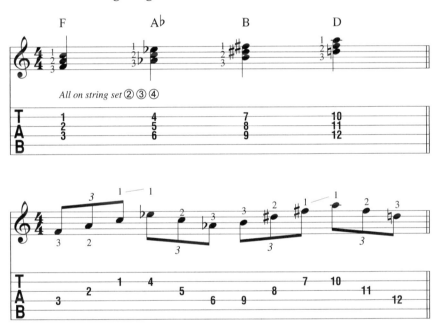

FIG. 4.5. Arpeggios

Try taking figure 4.5 and changing all the chords to minor, diminished, and finally, augmented chords, to fully understand the rationale here. (You will need to employ an open string on the F diminished chord.)

Triads and their arpeggios can also be played inversionally across the fingerboard, as well as moving by larger intervals with the chord in any position (root position, first inversion, and second inversion). Here's an example of root position major triads moving diagonally across the neck by the interval of a tritone.

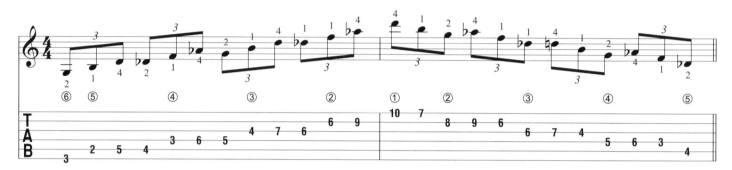

FIG. 4.6. Triads Moving by Tritones

Triad Anchors

Triads can be an "anchor" for organizing fingerings around. The A minor triad in figure 4.7 serves as a visual reference, location-wise, to plug in the scale fragments in bar 1, even though they infer E7 as far as harmonic function. The second bar resolves to A minor, and again, the bar's content can be fingered relative to the A minor shape.

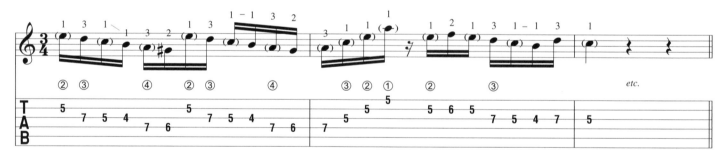

FIG. 4.7. Triads as Fingering Anchors

Seventh-Chord/Arpeggio Lines from Smart Boxes and Chords

Seventh-chord arpeggios/lines can be derived from portions of scales and chord shapes (smart boxes). This line comes primarily from the content of an A7 or A7(13) drop-2 voicing on the fifth fret.

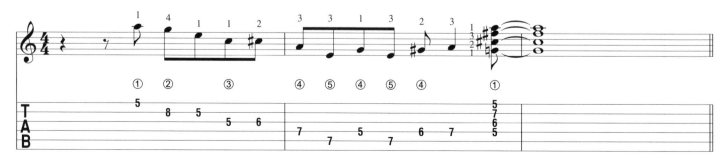

FIG. 4.8. Seventh-Chord Grip-Based Line

It's easy to see this next C7(9) jazz line coming from a Mixolydian scale fingering in second position (around the second fret). The chord shape in the last bar relates to the C7(9) arpeggio contained within the scale fingering. The first two beats of bar 1 are chromatic approaches to the root of the C7(9) chord.

FIG. 4.9. C7(9) Line from Mixolydian

Two Fingers Per String

Certain seventh chords like the diminished 7 can be easily played with two fingers per string diagonally up the fingerboard. Others are possible too, but some tend to be awkward.

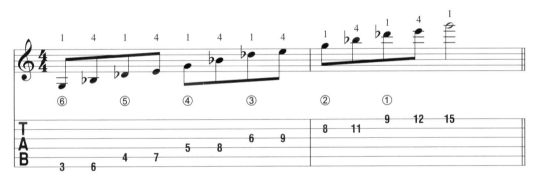

FIG. 4.10. Two Fingers Per String

Chromatic Approaches on the Same String

Chromatic approaches move into guide tones, triads, and seventh-chord outlines laterally on the same string.

A great component of bop-style improv language is chord outline with chromatics. I use this device frequently in the bop pieces here. Simple half-step approaches generally slide into a chord tone from the side. Sometimes, they are insertable within an outline's fingering. Other times, a longer stream of chromatics warrants some serious side-to-side movement into the outline:

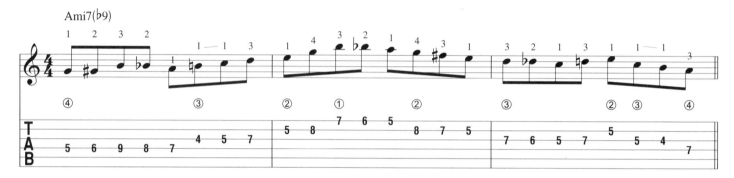

FIG. 4.11. Bop-Style Chromatic Fingerings

The idea here is to visualize the chord shape inside all of this. Sometimes, this creates some unusual fingerings, like in bar 1 with the root of the chord being played with the first finger, then jumping to an approach to the 3 of the chord with the same finger. Talk about non-sequential fingerings! But there are two mechanisms at work here: the uniform fingering of the double-sided (below and above) chromatic approach and the shape of the underlying chord shape/arpeggio. Passing scale notes are added for some balance and smoothing of the line. Practice this example until it becomes smooth and intuitive.

For a more in-depth study and organization of chromatic approaches, check out my book *The Practical Jazz Guitarist* (also published by Berklee Press).

Open Strings

Open strings are a great resource for fingering locations. They can be incorporated into a line to gain time to move location, or just help facilitate ease of playing content. When using open strings in lines, care needs to be taken in balancing the sound/duration of the open strings with the fretted notes. Use of open strings has been a big part of traditional classic guitar playing and repertoire. They also figure heavily in traditional American music styles (blues, open string guitar tunings, etc.), Brazilian guitar styles, and a whole lot more! I have utilized open string usage in the jazz and Bach pieces occasionally and particularly in "Fugue X."

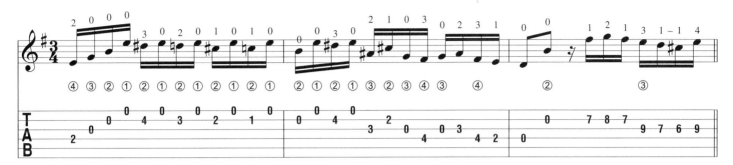

FIG. 4.12. Bach Line Utilizing Open Strings

Coltrane-Style Smart Boxes

Coltrane-esque scale fragments and chord pairings rendered on guitar are derived from "smart boxes." Modern jazz guitarists can't resist the musical gravitational pull, science, and influence of John Coltrane's music! Many contemporary compositions include chord sequences from his "Giant Steps" and "Countdown" pieces. And what guitarist among us hasn't wrangled with trying to get his solos down on the chromatic beast? Smart boxes are again a great resource to execute these building blocks of contemporary improv language Just locate a one-octave version (give or take) of the scale or chord arpeggio and move through the progression changing location to accommodate each chord. Here's an example which features scale fragment 1, 2, 3, 5 predominantly:

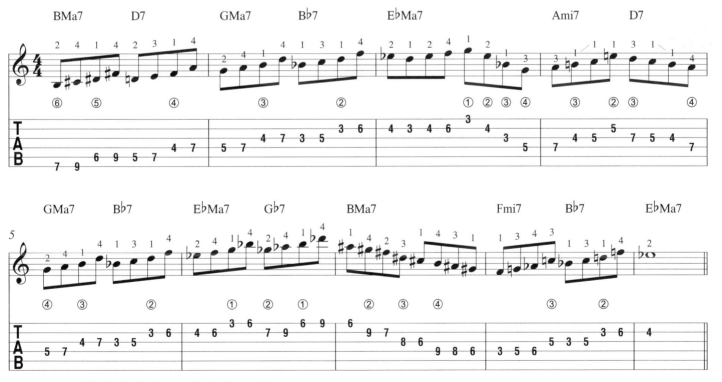

FIG. 4.13. Coltrane-Style Smart Boxes

Three-Finger Phrasing Style

Many self-taught guitarists don't use the "little finger" (pinky) when playing lines. We forget our first encounters with the guitar, the difficulty, and the physical trauma inflicted by trying to get the instrument together. Well, we forget that the pinky is initially weaker than the other fingers, and unless they are trained to use it, most folks won't! Of course, playing octaves and lots of chords need the little finger, so everybody does that, but the line playing by most self-taught players is pretty frequently done with three fingers.

Many players who "learn by ear" tend to physically cover more fingerboard territory in their fingering conception because they don't use the pinky. Wes Montgomery is a great example: Wes's lines move and cover a lot of fingerboard with his three-finger linear orientation. He also had an uncanny sense of guitaristic mechanics and musical connectivity. The result is a more vocal and horn-like quality line with a beautiful, swinging feel and impeccable musical timing. Of course, his octaves and chordal conception used all four fingers, and he turned the jazz guitar world upside-down with his amazing playing! Wes will be remembered forever!

Many of us started out with teachers who advocated for the use of scales in our studies. Any guitarist attending music school will work on scales. Scales are great and useful for a number of reasons, but one thing is for sure: scales help you to develop that little finger.

So, use the fourth finger where it's useful and logical for you. Experiment with the three-finger phrase. Use this concept to expand your guitar navigation and phrasing, and apply where appropriate. You'll find many examples of both conceptions in the fingerings on these pages.

A Shopping List for Fingering Proficiency

Knowing and understanding musical content makes us more aware of where to play things when we encounter them. Berklee guitar students take a "proficiency test" every semester that keeps them acquiring a knowledge base of practical, usable resources to organize the guitar fingerboard. It's a worthwhile endeavor for any good musician. So here's a short list of "proficiency materials" we teach at Berklee that will aid you in organizing the guitar fingerboard. Become "proficient" in their content, execution, and usage!

Scales

Major, melodic minor, harmonic minor, harmonic major scales: these are all seven-tone scales, and should be played in all keys. All modal scales derived from these "master" seven-tone scales should be practiced as well. Non-seven-tone scales to learn include chromatic, whole tone, diminished, pentatonic, and blues scale. All scales/modes should be played in one-octave, two-octave, and three-octave configurations. In-position (across), three notes per string (diagonal), and on a single string (lateral) should all be explored.

Arpeggios

- **Triads:** major, minor, diminished, augmented. Learn one-, two-, and three-octave configurations, as well as on a single string at a time, from the root and in all inversions.

- **Seventh chords:** Ma7, Ma7♯5, Ma7♭5, mi7, mi7♭5, mi/Ma7, °7, dom7, 7♯5, 7♭5, 7sus4. One-, two-, and three-octave configurations, as well as on a single string at a time, from the root and in all inversions.

Chords

- **Triads:** major, minor, diminished, augmented. Played across and laterally using string groups in closed and open position from and through all chord positions (root, first, and second inversions), as well as both closed and spread (open) through all cycles diatonic to major, melodic minor, harmonic minor, and harmonic major scales.

- **Seventh chords:** Ma7, Ma7♯5, Ma7♭5, mi7, mi7♭5, mi/Ma7, °7, dom7, 7♯5, 7♭5, 7sus4. Drop 2 and drop 3 all chord types eventually voice-led through all inversions from a given chord position.

This is just a very short list to start putting together that doesn't even touch on quartal harmony, artificial scales, etc. There's always a lot more to learn, but this is a good start.

PART II

From Bach to Bebop

The etudes in this section include a Bach piece and a jazz piece that are in the same key (at least initially!) and frequently utilize many of the same harmonies and progressions typical to both genres. My original pieces are all dedicated to amazing musicians and teachers with whom I've had the honor to study, and in most cases, to perform with. These musicians had a huge impact on my musical development and for so many others. So, this is kind of my "homage" to these superlative musicians who have contributed so much to the relatively young art of jazz performance and jazz education. Perhaps in the years to come, one will be able to trace the future's jazz artists back to them in a timeline spanning hundreds of years, like the classical traditions do.

In the jazz pieces, many musical phrases and ideas repeat, in order to draw your attention to them. Sometimes, too much diverse information has a hard time being digested and assimilated. Better to use more repetitive material that sticks to your ribs for later use! For instance, you'll find many variations of what I like to call the "snap."

Fig. II.1. The Snap

This figure has a pushing kind of momentum that adds drive to a line. The wrong fingering can turn it into mush. So learn it well; it's ubiquitous and useful in all jazz repertoire!

There's sometimes a series of chords mixed with the line. This is a great "Jim Hall" device that breaks up a line, but also reminds the player of the harmonies at hand. You'll find this device in the Bach, too.

Most of all, the pieces—Bach and jazz (and this book in general)—are about getting sensible, logical fingerings on the guitar fingerboard that relate to the harmony or to connecting harmonies.

Again, remember the bop saw: *The line is the chord, and the chord is the line.*

5. Bach "Fugue I" in C Major and "Pollo Arrosto Suite"

Bach "Fugue I" in C Major

This Bach piece, like the "Prelude XVII" (see chapter 9), is based on a strong motif (part of the fugue's "subject") that incorporates a recurring secondal idea.

FIG. 5.1. Motif

Here is the full subject:

FIG. 5.2. Full Subject

The fingering for the motif should be on a single string. It's almost always comprised of a major second, so it should always be fingered with 1 to 3, in all its various transpositions. (The exception is in guitar III, beginning in bar 22, when it's a half-step fingering 1-2.) This motif acts as a kind of "anchor" to build the other fingerings around.

Speaking of fingerings, this piece poses some real challenges due to the high register of the first part. The entire piece is transposed up an octave from the original keyboard manuscript to keep all the content in balance. Obviously, this gets into the highest notes available on most fingerboards, which creates a couple of issues. First, it's just plain hard squeezing your fingers into those little slots at the end of the fingerboard. And second, it's hard to get the notes to ring when there's only a third of the string length left to vibrate.

So, when you're at the highest of the notes, sometimes there are very few options, location-wise. When the register drops a bit, I try to move back down the fingerboard to get some "ring" into the notes. In some instances, one has to make a leap in register to connect content, especially on the same string. I tend to use my third finger for this. It's stronger and a little more "sure-footed" than using the pinky.

Incorporate these ideas into your own fingerings. Write them in pencil, as you're likely to change your mind after living with the pieces awhile....

An additional note for this piece: There's one particularly high-register trill in Guitar I that many guitarists won't easily be able to reach on a "standard" twenty-fret fingerboard. It's a Baroque-style trill starting on the upper neighbor tone. You could skip it, if it's too high, but on a modern instrument, you might be able to catch it.

This C major fugue is paired with "Pollo Arrosto Suite," based on Charlie Parker's "Yardbird Suite."

Fugue I

J.S. Bach

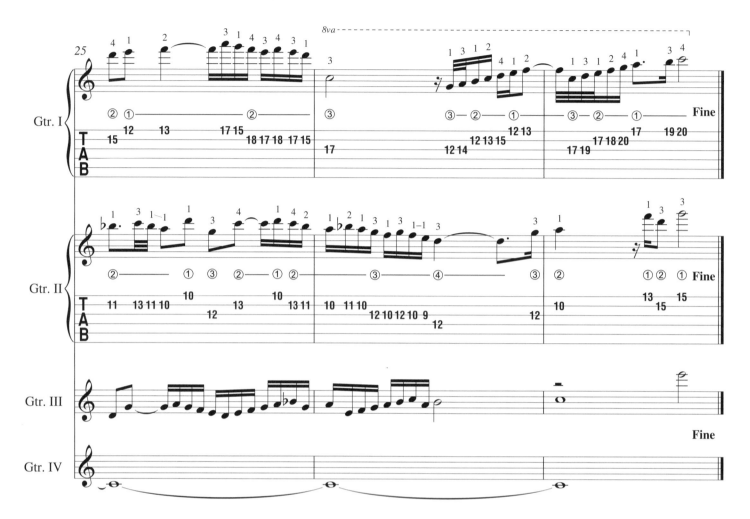

FIG. 5.3. Bach "Fugue I" in C Major

Pollo Arrosto Suite

"Pollo Arrosto" was written for my good friend Garrison Fewell. A wonderful guitarist and teacher who questioned convention and created great musical beauty on the guitar, Garrison was a constant seeker of wisdom. He was on the Berklee guitar faculty for thirty-seven years, and his books are widely used by guitarists the world over. The piece is based on Charlie Parker's "Yardbird Suite" and is paired with the Bach "Fugue I" in C major.

Pollo Arrosto Suite

for Garrison Fewell

Mark White

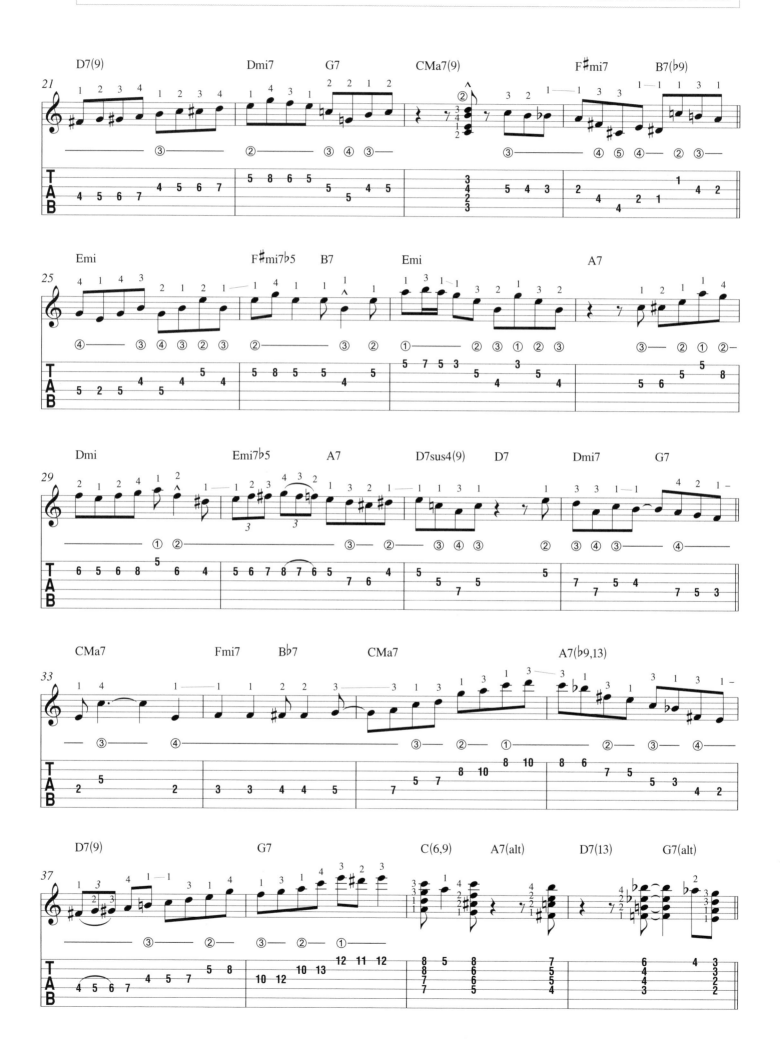

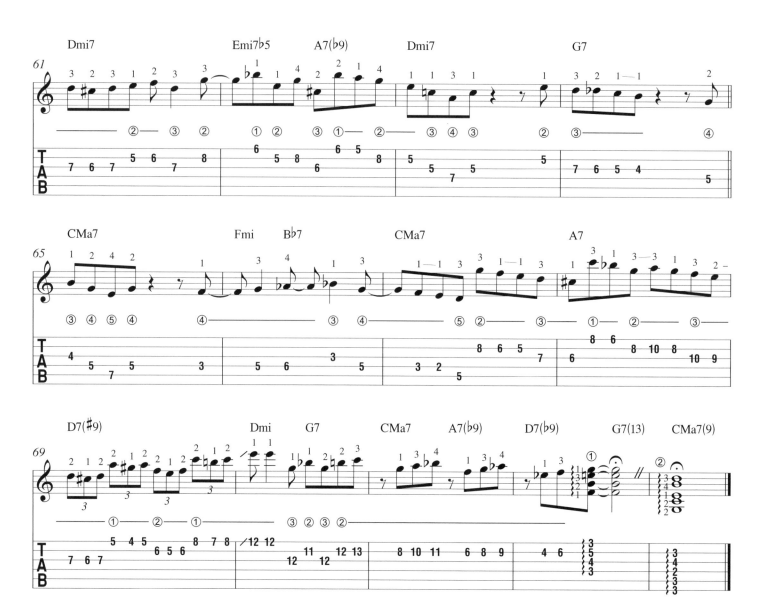

FIG. 5.4. Pollo Arrosto Suite

6. Bach "Prelude II" in C Minor and "I Hear a Blasphemy"

Bach "Prelude II" in C Minor

This is a great piece and a lot of fun to play! It's definitely chord oriented, whether you follow one part or the sum total of both together. Just follow the harmonies (sometimes harmonic fragments) under your fingers, and you'll be on the right track.

All four fingers do yeoman's duty throughout this piece, and this is a great study in finger independence. The first two thirds of the piece pretty much features a new change (chord) by bar that is repeated within each measure, and every finger takes a turn beginning and orienting within the various bars throughout the piece.

An interesting "twist" arose while I was creating this arrangement. I found that at certain times, the best orientation for me was to move into the harmonies leading primarily with the first two fingers, when possible. Bar 2, part 1 is a perfect example, and this happens frequently.

Even when all the fingers are employed, there's still a great emphasis on 1–2 fingering. It becomes a point of focus, as you will see. I think of this piece as the Django Reinhardt etude, due to this fingering disposition.

In addition, there is some interesting finger shifting employed that really adds to the *moto perpetuo* vibe, as well as great use of sequence employed from bar 28 onwards. These sequences feature fingerings moving (primarily) down in string groups, which help to visualize content, aid consistency, and improve technique, as well as enhancing phrasing. Bars 25–27 can be played by both parts or by either one.

In the notation here and elsewhere in this book, the fingerings have been simplified due to the repetitious quality of the piece. Just one string is marked per group of notes, in the first section. It won't be hard to figure out the other strings! The note groupings repeat too, so this is a way to simplify the notation, to let you focus on the music.

8–12

This prelude is paired with "I Hear a Blasphemy," based on a classic jazz progression.

Prelude II

J.S. Bach

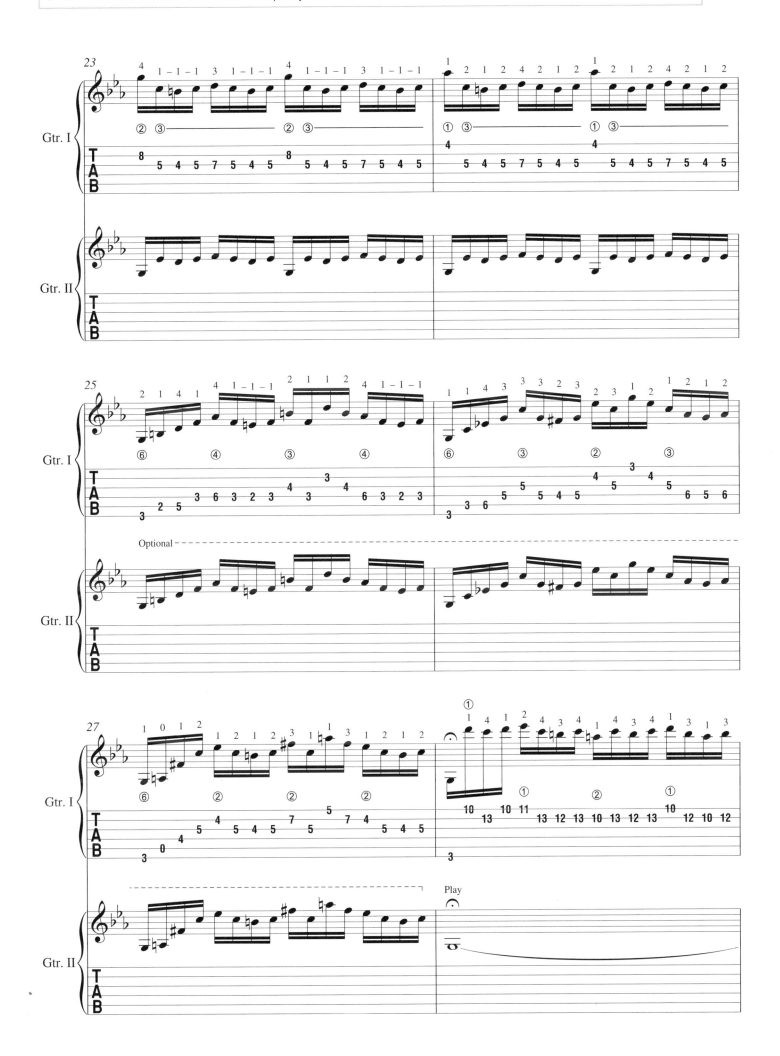

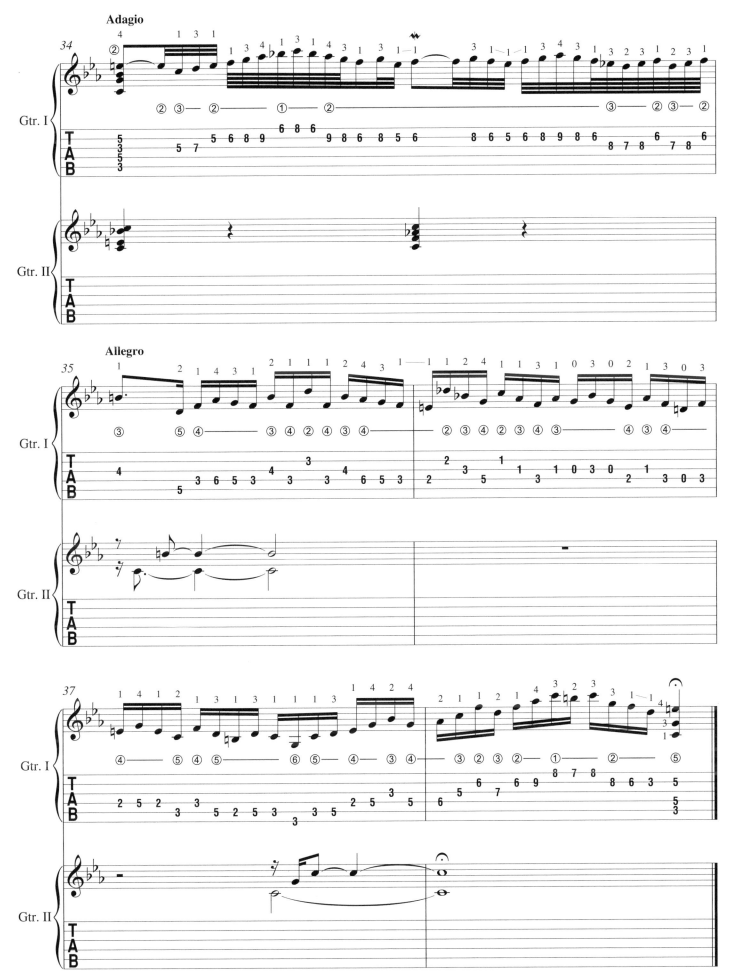

FIG. 6.1. Bach "Prelude II" in C Minor

I Hear a Blasphemy

"I Hear a Blasphemy" was written for Herb Pomeroy, a monumental performer and one of the earliest and greatest jazz pedagogues who ever lived. His big band and small groups ruled Boston. Herb's arranging and analysis of Ellington and line writing concepts influenced generations of musicians and helped put Berklee on the map. A true genius.

13–14

"I Hear a Blasphemy" is based on one of my favorite standard tunes, "I Hear a Rhapsody." It's paired with the Bach "Prelude II" in C minor.

I Hear a Blasphemy
for Herb Pomeroy

Mark White

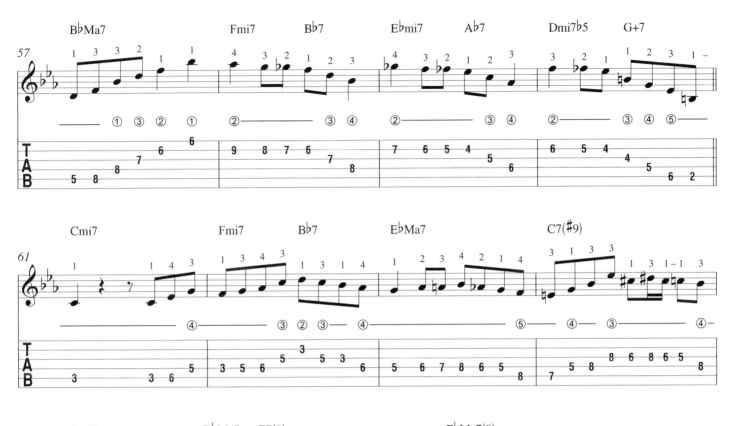

FIG. 6.2. I Hear a Blasphemy

7. Bach "Prelude V" in D Major and "Tsunami Mommy"

Bach "Prelude V" in D Major

This piece is a real challenge due to the non-stop nature of the first part. Implied harmonies form the basis for fingerings, but there's a special factor that I key into to find fingerings. Interestingly, it's the shape of a minor seventh interval, which tends to fall on beat 4, in the first two sixteenths.

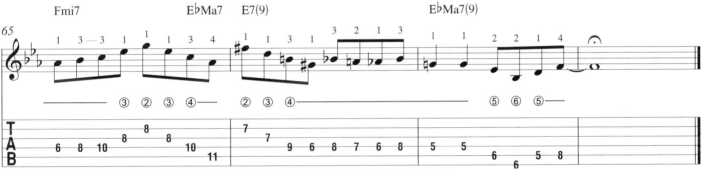

FIG. 7.1. Minor Seventh

Occasionally, the interval here is a major seventh, a major sixth, a ninth, or a fourth, and sometimes it happens on another beat other than 4. But the majority of occurrences are on beat 4, first two sixteenths, and they are predominantly minor seventh intervals. Most of the time, fingers 1 and 2 do it (sometimes 3 and 4), but it depends on the string group; sometimes, the first finger plays both notes, depending on the interval and string group, but sometimes an open string is employed. (There's a long bout of in-position fingerings utilized at bar 19 taking advantage of the open D string.) The main thing is to latch onto this occurrence when it happens, and use it to inform your fingering choices.

Guitar II is mainly a chord-tone line supporting Guitar I. Because of the easier nature of this part, it is played with drop D tuning to preserve some of the low end. Drop D tunings are fairly common. Johnny Smith tuned his guitar with a low drop D, and Andrés Segovia used it frequently in his transcriptions—notably, the Bach "Chaconne" in D minor, which is a great example. It takes a little getting used to, adjusting the other notes up a couple more frets, but proceedings are simple enough in the second part and the musical results are worth it.

"Prelude V" is paired with "Tsunami Mommy," based on the changes of Antonio Carlos Jobim's "Wave."

15–19

Prelude V

J.S. Bach

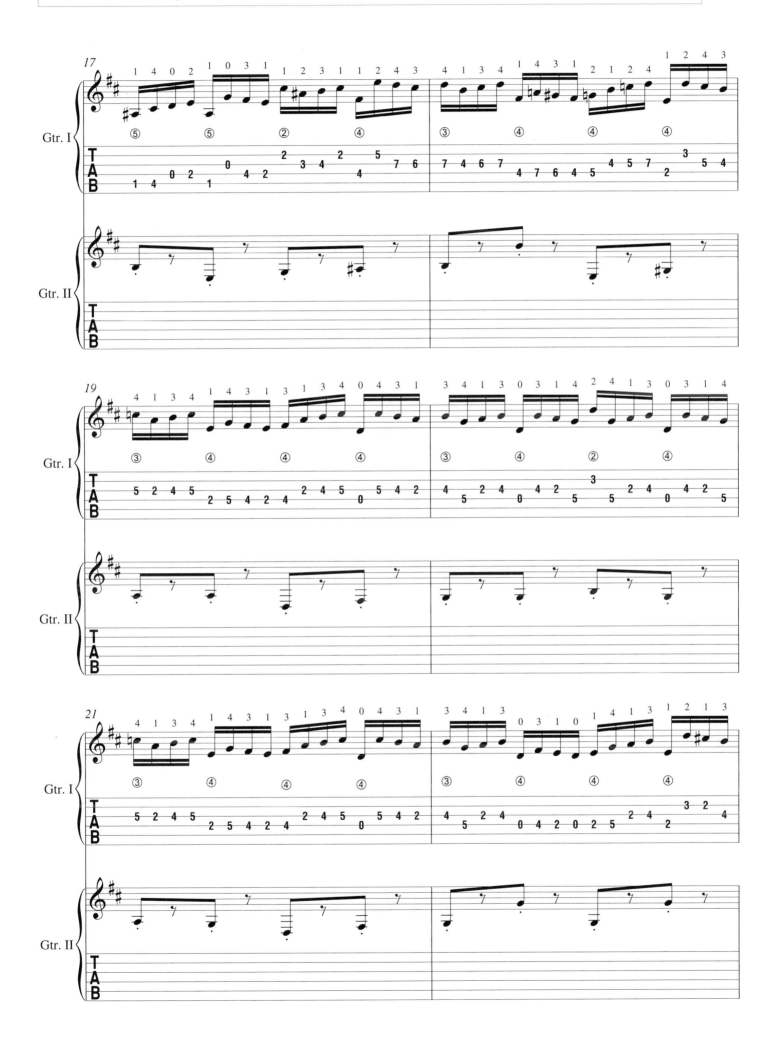

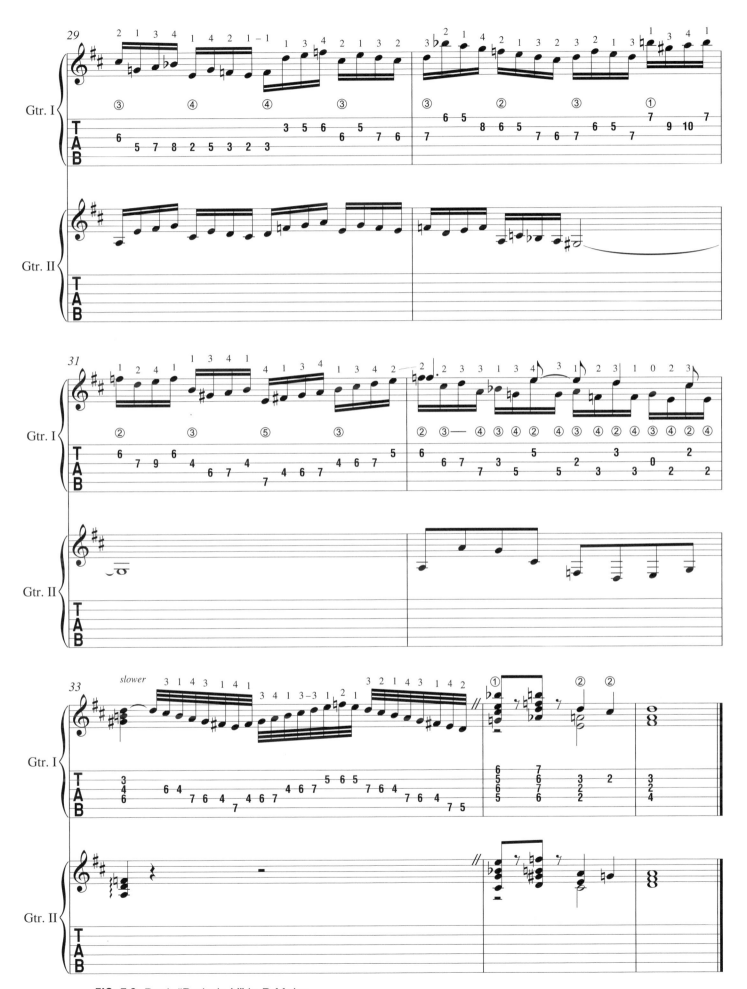

FIG. 7.2. Bach "Prelude V" in D Major

Tsunami Mommy

"Tsunami Mommy" was written for the great jazz guitarist and a personal hero for me, Joe Negri. Joe is a real-life Pittsburgh music legend. The most workin' guitarist in town and a real class act! He's worked everywhere and with everyone. Joe was a true role model for many of us coming out of Pittsburgh. His mild-mannered T.V. façade that many knew him by disguised a consummate professional, burning jazz guitar player! "Tsunami Mommy" is based on a classic bossa nova tune in D major and paired with the Bach "Prelude V."

20–21

Tsunami Mommy
for Joe Negri

Mark White

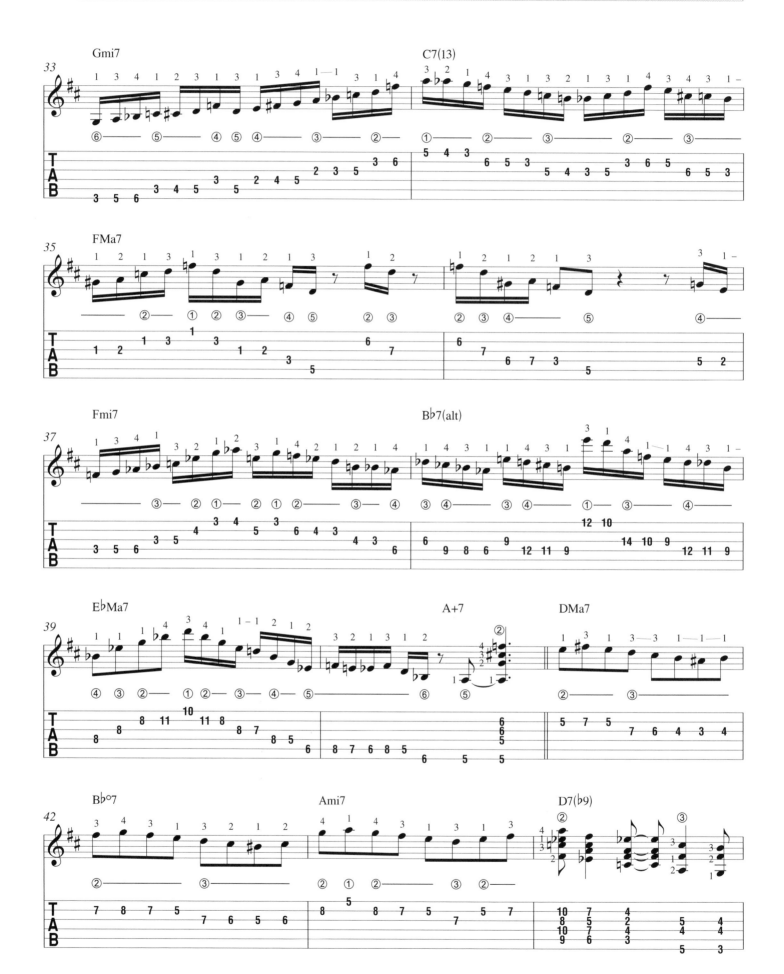

FIG. 7.3. Tsunami Mommy

8. Bach "Fugue X" in E Minor and "Sidranopolis"

Bach "Fugue X" in E Minor

The Bach "Fugue X" in E minor features use of open strings *sostenuto* style. Either a held chord, arpeggiated, or a moving line played against an open, ringing string imparts a "classical guitar" sound. The two parts are staggered in canon fashion as a kind of musical chase, followed by some two-part lines in thirds and sixths that will be sure to satisfy any Allman Brothers fan! More trading and some additional open-string passages complete this very enjoyable piece of music.

Octave adjustments are employed in the low part, for clarity, but the majority of the high part is played where written for keyboard, the lower octave and use of open strings creating a full, rich sound. "Fugue X" is paired with "Sidranopolis," based on a well-known jazz progression.

Fugue X

J.S. Bach

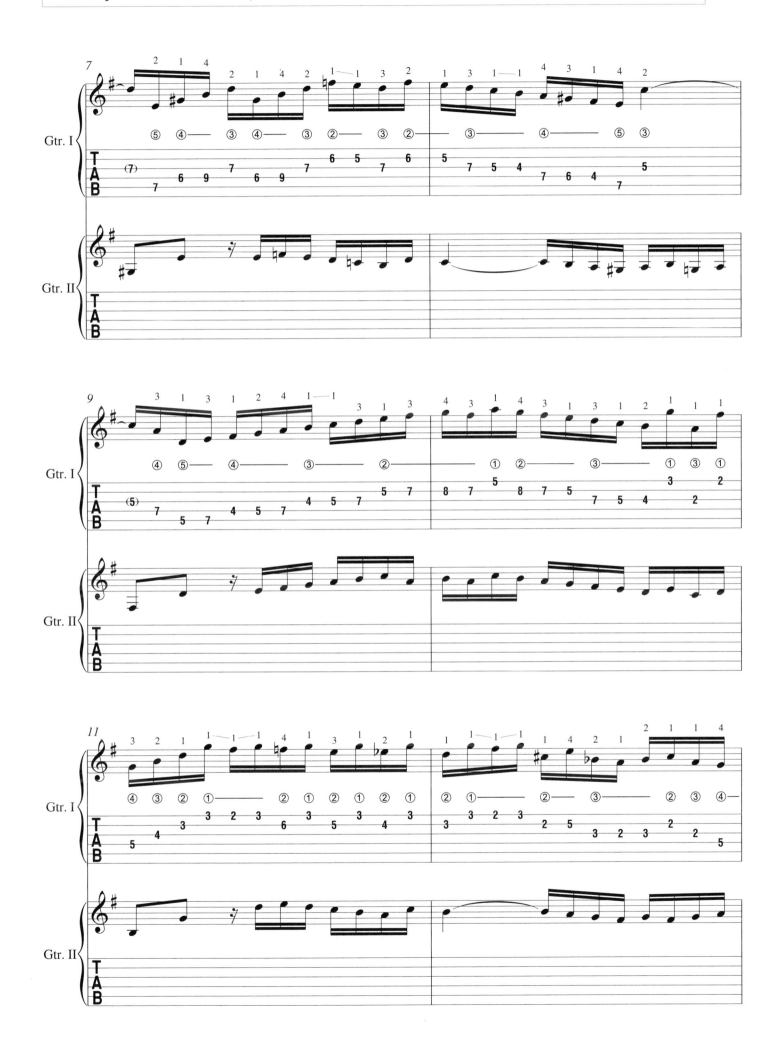

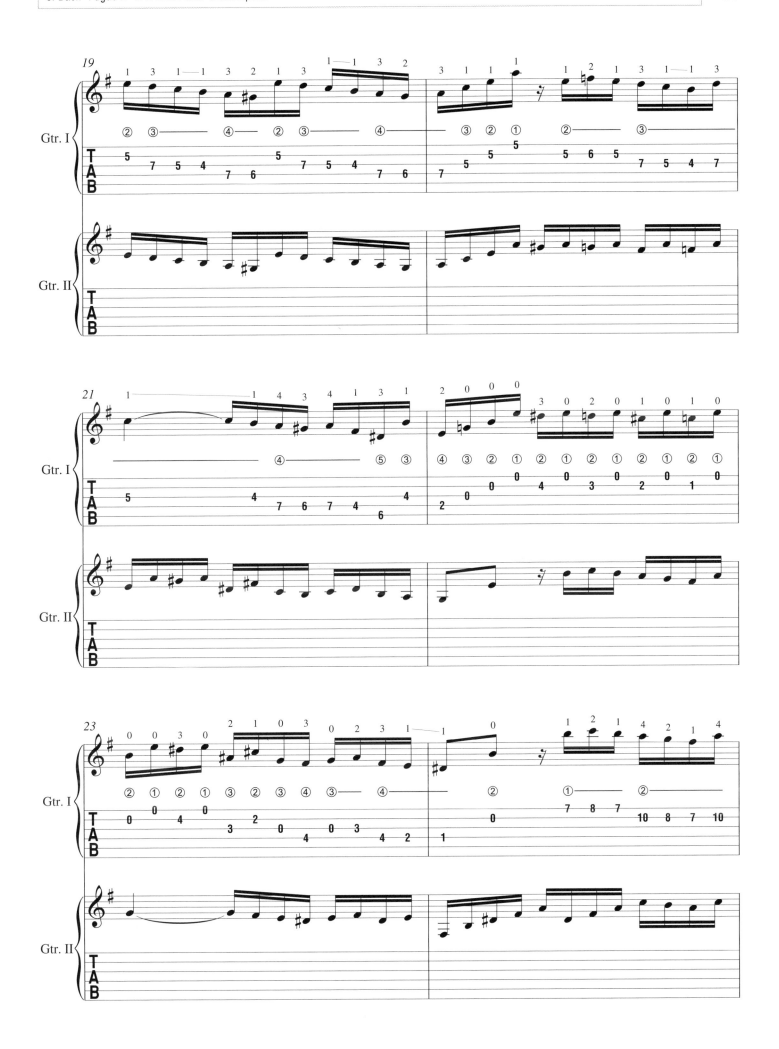

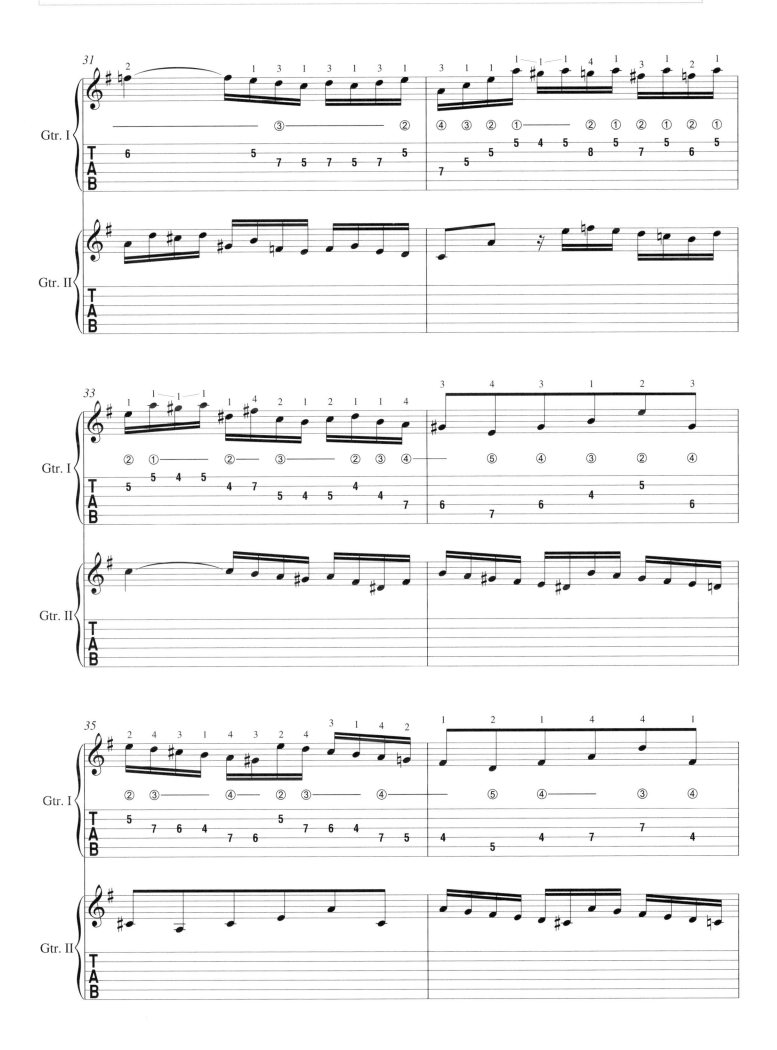

FIG. 8.1. Bach "Fugue X" in E Minor

Sidranopolis

"Sidranopolis" is dedicated to Charlie Banacos. Charlie was one of the greatest jazz pedagogues and jazz pianists of all time. Charlie was a true genius, creating paths to developing each student's potential on a one-to-one basis. Solid as Gibraltar in all facets of piano performance, composition, and piano repertoire, he was especially well versed in Bach. One of Charlie's great heroes was pianist Bill Evans, who probably wrote the tune "Nardis" that "Sidranopolis" is based on, although it's often credited to Miles Davis. "Sidranopolis" features the use of open strings as found in the Bach "Fugue X" in E Minor.

Sidranopolis

for Charlie Banacos

Mark White

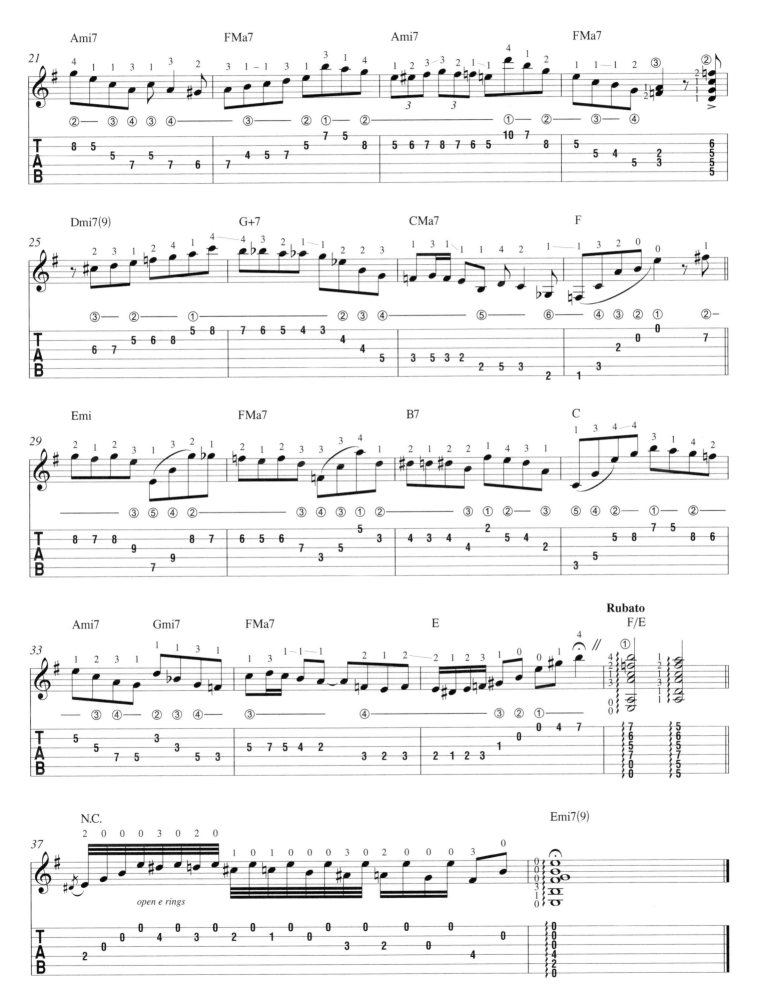

FIG. 8.2. Sidranopolis

9. Bach "Prelude XVII" in A♭ Major and "Wiglaf's in da Bag"

Bach "Prelude XVII" in A♭ Major

This Bach prelude is heavily based on this recurring rhythmic motif:

FIG. 9.1. Motif (and Variation)

The motif moves through many sequences/harmonies that infer standard jazz chords and progressions, many of which can be found in the pairing piece "Wiglaf's in da Bag" (on a standard jazz progression). The two sixteenth notes in the motif are always constructed of a major second or minor second interval before moving into the arpeggio formed by the remaining eighth notes in the motif. The first sixteenth note is always a part of the chord, and the second sixteenth is a scalar or chromatic approach note. Bach was boppin' and outlining changes three hundred years ago!

The minor and major seconds are usually played on the same string, usually using fingers 1–2 or 1–3. This builds in an automatic and organic location system that gets a good clean attack and is easier to visualize on the fingerboard. The following arpeggio moves as dictated by the two-sixteenths' location.

In a couple of spots, open strings simplify the maneuvers. The trills in part I sometimes dictate playing longer groups of notes on one string.

I also like to use the three-finger phrasing previously discussed (see chapter 4). There are usually alternate fingerings given in these situations. See if you can "echo" the ideas here in your fingering of part II.

Prelude XVII

29–33

J.S. Bach

FIG. 9.2. Bach "Prelude XVII" in A♭ Major

Wiglaf's in da Bag

"Wiglaf's in da Bag" is dedicated to Joe Pass, an absolute icon of jazz guitar. He will always be remembered as a musical force. Joe created a veritable mountain of jazz art to learn from and enjoy. He also generously took some time to work with me, and I'd like to pass on some of his ideas. "Wiglaf's in da Bag" is based on a well-known jazz progression and is paired with Bach's "Prelude XVII."

Wiglaf's in da Bag
for Joe Pass

Mark White

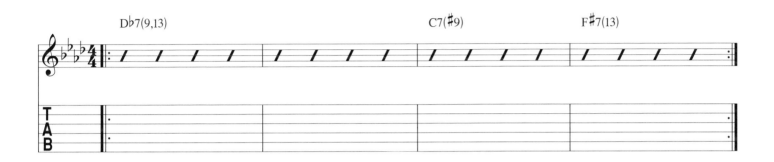

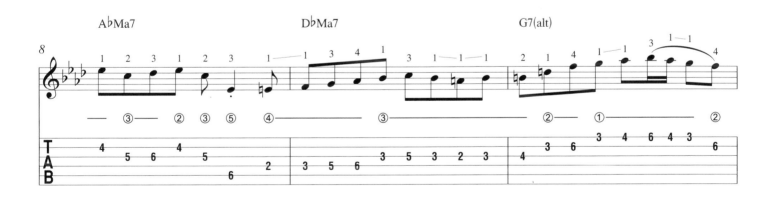

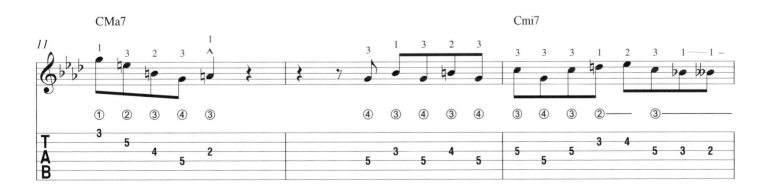

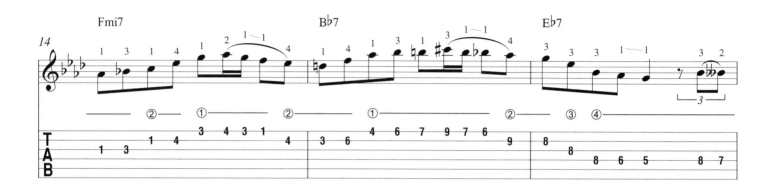

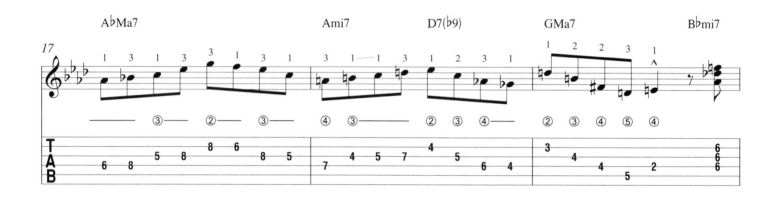

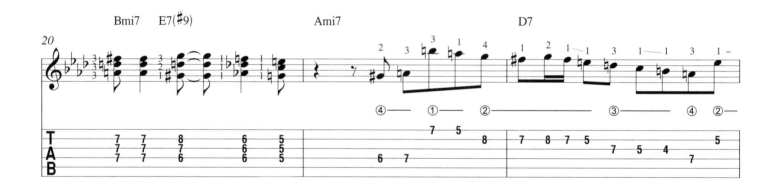

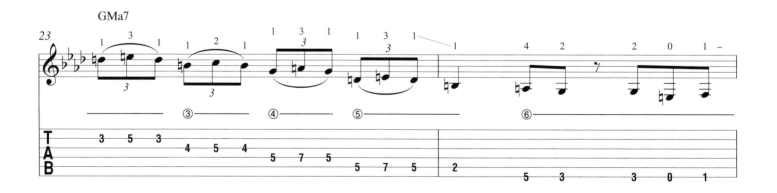

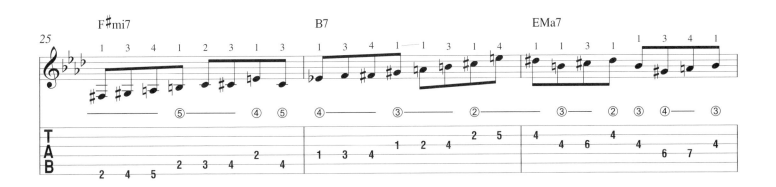

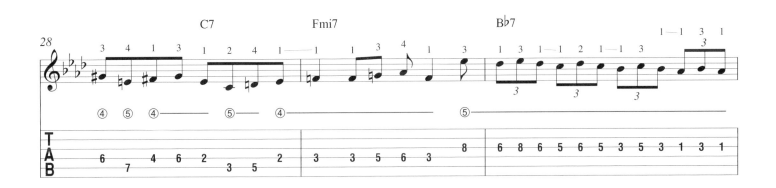

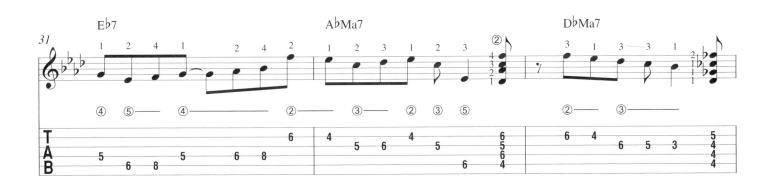

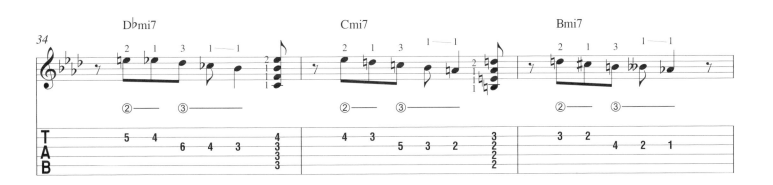

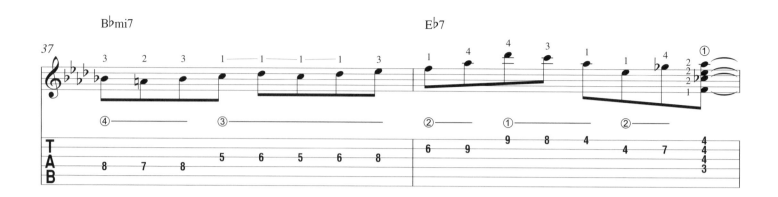

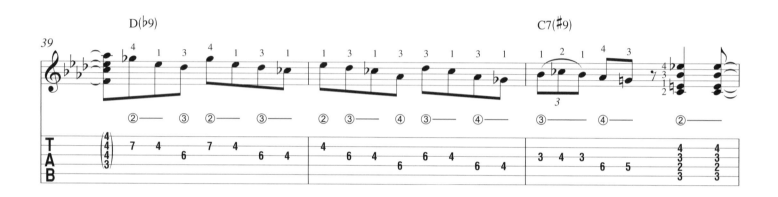

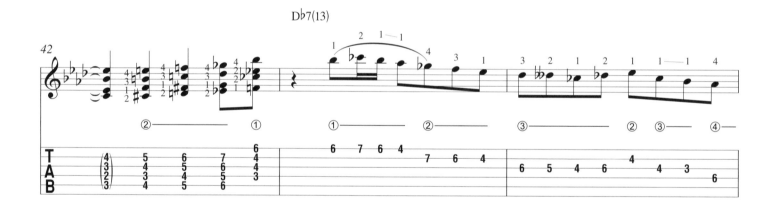

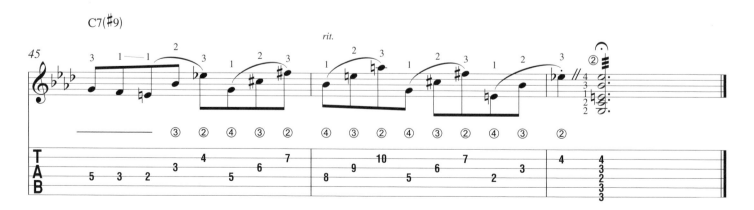

FIG. 9.2. Wiglaf's in da Bag

ABOUT THE AUTHOR

Mark White is a performing jazz guitarist and educator, who has worked in various professional capacities with artists such as George Russell's Living Time Orchestra, Gil Evans, John McNeil, Paul Broadnax, Herb Pomeroy, Larry Monroe, Victor Mendoza, Ken Peplowski, the Kenny Hadley Big Band, John Allmark Jazz Orchestra, the Boston Pops, the Bebop Guitars, Boston Musica Viva, and Last Trip. He has performed with dozens of major touring theatre shows and theater personalities in the New England area, done extensive studio/production work for widely diverse recorded projects, and participated in over fifty road trips/clinics/performances for Berklee College of Music since the early 1990s. He has made recordings for Blue Note, King, MMC records, Heineken Jazz Festival, and Grescotmar Ltd. productions.

Performances as a featured jazz artist at major concert venues include Lincoln Center, Coolidge Auditorium at the Library of Congress, the Smithsonian, Wolf Trap, and many major venues in the northeast and music festivals across the United States, Canada, and in fifteen other countries across the globe, including at the Umbria Jazz Festival, Settembre Musicale, Tokyo Music Joy, Maré de Agosto, and the Heineken Jazz Festival in Puerto Rico, to name a few.

Mark holds a bachelor's degree and master's degree in music from the New England Conservatory and has studied with Joe Negri, Joe Pass, Jack Wilkins, Gene Bertoncini, Herb Pomeroy, Jaki Byard, George Russell, William Thomas McKinley, Jerry Bergonzi, and Charlie Banacos. Mark is a jazz educator with over thirty years experience in the field. Currently a senior professor of guitar at Berklee College of Music, he has published three books: *Bach Chorales for Guitar Quartet* for Mark S. Henry Music, *Advanced Reading Etudes* for Grescotmar Ltd. publications, and most recently, *The Practical Jazz Guitarist* for Berklee Press/Hal Leonard Publishing.

INDEX

More Fine Publications

Berklee Press

GUITAR

BEBOP GUITAR SOLOS
by Michael Kaplan
00121703 Book..........................$14.99

BLUES GUITAR TECHNIQUE
by Michael Williams
50449623 Book/Online Audio...........$24.99

BERKLEE GUITAR CHORD DICTIONARY
by Rick Peckham
50449546 Jazz - Book.......................$10.99
50449596 Rock - Book.......................$12.99

THE CHORD FACTORY
by Jon Damian
50449541 Book...........................$24.95

CLASSICAL TECHNIQUE FOR THE MODERN GUITARIST
by Kim Perlak
00148781 Book/Online Audio.............$19.99

CONTEMPORARY JAZZ GUITAR SOLOS
by Michael Kaplan
00143596 ....$16.99

CREATIVE CHORDAL HARMONY FOR GUITAR
by Mick Goodrick and Tim Miller
50449613 Book/Online Audio.............$19.99

FUNK/R&B GUITAR
by Thaddeus Hogarth
50449569 Book/CD $19.95

GUITAR CHOP SHOP – BUILDING ROCK/METAL TECHNIQUE
by Joe Stump
50449601 Book/Online Audio............$19.99

INTRODUCTION TO JAZZ GUITAR
by Jane Miller
00125041 Book/Online Audio.............$19.99

JAZZ GUITAR FRETBOARD NAVIGATION
by Mark White
00154107 Book/Online Audio.............$19.99

JAZZ IMPROVISATION FOR GUITAR
by Garrison Fewell
A Harmonic Approach
50449594 Book/CD $24.99
A Melodic Approach
50449503 Book/CD...........................$24.99

JAZZ SWING GUITAR
by Jon Wheatley
00139935 Book/Online Audio............$19.99

A MODERN METHOD FOR GUITAR*
by William Leavitt
Volume 1: Beginner
00137387 Book/Online Video...........$24.99
**Other volumes, media options, and supporting songbooks available.*

THE PRIVATE GUITAR STUDIO HANDBOOK
by Michael McAdam
00121641 Book...........................$14.99

BASS

BASS LINES
Fingerstyle Funk
by Joe Santerre
50449542 Book/CD $19.95
Metal
by David Marvuglio
00122465 Book/Online Audio............$19.99
Rock
by Joe Santerre
50449478 Book/CD $19.95

BERKLEE JAZZ BASS
by Rich Appleman, Whit Browne, and Bruce Gertz
50449636 Book/Online Audio...........$19.99

FUNK BASS FILLS
by Anthony Vitti
50449608 Book/CD $19.99

INSTANT BASS
by Danny Morris
50449502 Book/CD $14.95

DRUMS

BEGINNING DJEMBE
by Michael Markus & Joe Galeota
00148210 Book/Online Video $16.99

DOUBLE BASS DRUM INTEGRATION
by Henrique De Almeida
00120208 Book...........................$19.99

DRUM SET WARM-UPS
by Rod Morgenstein
50449465 Book...........................$12.99

DRUM STUDIES
by Dave Vose
50449617 Book...........................$12.99

EIGHT ESSENTIALS OF DRUMMING
by Ron Savage
50448048 Book/CD $19.99

PHRASING: ADVANCED RUDIMENTS FOR CREATIVE DRUMMING
by Russ Gold
00120209 Book...........................$19.99

WORLD JAZZ DRUMMING
by Mark Walker
50449568 Book/CD $22.99

PIANO/KEYBOARD

BERKLEE JAZZ KEYBOARD HARMONY
by Suzanna Sifter
00138874 Book/Online Audio............$24.99

BERKLEE JAZZ PIANO
by Ray Santisi
50448047 Book/CD $19.99

CHORD-SCALE IMPROVISATION FOR KEYBOARD
by Ross Ramsay
50449597 Book/CD...........................$19.99

CONTEMPORARY PIANO TECHNIQUE
by Stephany Tiernan
50449545 Book/DVD $29.99

HAMMOND ORGAN COMPLETE
by Dave Limina
50449479 Book/CD.........................$24.95

JAZZ PIANO COMPING
by Suzanne Davis
50449614 Book/CD $19.99

LATIN JAZZ PIANO IMPROVISATION
by Rebecca Cline
50449649 Book/CD.........................$24.99

SOLO JAZZ PIANO – 2ND ED.
by Neil Olmstead
50449641 Book/CD...........................$39.99

VOICE

BELTING
by Jeannie Gagné
00124984 Book/Online Media............$19.99

THE CONTEMPORARY SINGER – 2ND ED.
by Anne Peckham
50449595 Book/CD $24.99

TIPS FOR SINGERS
by Carolyn Wilkins
50449557 Book/CD.........................$19.95

VOCAL TECHNIQUE
featuring Anne Peckham
50448038 DVD.............................$19.95

VOCAL WORKOUTS FOR THE CONTEMPORARY SINGER
by Anne Peckham
50448044 Book/CD $24.95

YOUR SINGING VOICE
by Jeannie Gagné
50449619 Book/CD $29.99

WOODWINDS/BRASS

FAMOUS SAXOPHONE SOLOS
arr. Jeff Harrington
50449605 Book...........................$14.99

FLUTE SOUND EFFECTS
by Ueli Dörig
00128980 Book/Online Audio............$16.99

THE SAXOPHONE HANDBOOK
by Douglas D. Skinner
50449658 Book...........................$14.99

SAXOPHONE SOUND EFFECTS
by Ueli Dörig
50449628 Book/CD $15.99

TRUMPET SOUND EFFECTS
by Craig Pedersen and Ueli Dörig
00121626 Book/Online Audio.............$14.99

Berklee Press Publications feature material
developed at the Berklee College of Music.
To browse the complete Berklee Press Catalog, go to
www.berkleepress.com

ROOTS MUSIC/STRINGS

BERKLEE HARP
Chords, Styles, and Improvisation for Pedal and Lever Harp
by Felice Pomeranz
00144263 Book/Online Audio $19.99

BEYOND BLUEGRASS
Beyond Bluegrass Banjo
by Dave Hollander and Matt Glaser
50449610 Book/CD $19.99

Beyond Bluegrass Mandolin
by John McGann and Matt Glaser
50449609 Book/CD $19.99

Bluegrass Fiddle and Beyond
by Matt Glaser
50449602 Book/CD $19.99

EXPLORING CLASSICAL MANDOLIN
by August Watters
00125040 Book/Online Media $19.99

FIDDLE TUNES ON JAZZ CHANGES
by Matt Glaser
00120210 Book/Online Audio $16.99

THE IRISH CELLO BOOK
by Liz Davis Maxfield
50449652 Book/CD $24.99

JAZZ UKULELE
by Abe Lagrimas, Jr.
00121624 Book/Online Audio $19.99

BERKLEE PRACTICE METHOD

GET YOUR BAND TOGETHER
With additional volumes for other instruments, plus a teacher's guide.
Bass
by Rich Appleman, John Repucci and the Berklee Faculty
50449427 Book/CD $14.95

Drum Set
by Ron Savage, Casey Scheuerell and the Berklee Faculty
50449429 Book/CD $14.95

Guitar
by Larry Baione and the Berklee Faculty
50449426 Book/CD $16.99

Keyboard
by Russell Hoffmann, Paul Schmeling and the Berklee Faculty
50449428 Book/CD $14.95

WELLNESS

MANAGE YOUR STRESS AND PAIN THROUGH MUSIC
by Dr. Suzanne B. Hanser and Dr. Susan E. Mandel
50449592 Book/CD $29.99

MUSICIAN'S YOGA
by Mia Olson
50449587 Book $14.99

THE NEW MUSIC THERAPIST'S HANDBOOK – SECOND ED.
by Dr. Suzanne B. Hanser
50449424 Book $29.95

MUSIC THEORY/EAR TRAINING/ IMPROVISATION

BEGINNING EAR TRAINING
by Gilson Schachnik
50449548 Book/CD $16.99

THE BERKLEE BOOK OF JAZZ HARMONY
by Joe Mulholland & Tom Hojnacki
00113755 Book/CD $24.99

BERKLEE MUSIC THEORY – 2ND ED.
by Paul Schmeling
Rhythm, Scales Intervals
50449615 Book/Online Audio $24.99
Harmony
50449616 Book/CD............................. $22.99

IMPROVISATION FOR CLASSICAL MUSICIANS
by Eugene Friesen with Wendy M. Friesen
50449637 Book/CD $24.99

REHARMONIZATION TECHNIQUES
by Randy Felts
50449496 Book..................................... $29.95

MUSIC BUSINESS

HOW TO GET A JOB IN THE MUSIC INDUSTRY – 3RD EDITION
by Keith Hatschek with Breanne Beseda
00130699 Book..................................... $27.99

MAKING MUSIC MAKE MONEY
by Eric Beall
50448009 Book $26.95

MUSIC INDUSTRY FORMS
by Jonathan Feist
00121814 Book $14.99

MUSIC MARKETING
by Mike King
50449588 Book..................................... $24.99

PROJECT MANAGEMENT FOR MUSICIANS
by Jonathan Feist
50449659 Book..................................... $27.99

THE SELF-PROMOTING MUSICIAN – 3RD EDITION
by Peter Spellman
00119607 Book..................................... $24.99

MUSIC PRODUCTION & ENGINEERING

AUDIO MASTERING
by Jonathan Wyner
50449581 Book/CD.............................. $29.99

AUDIO POST PRODUCTION
by Mark Cross
50449627 Book..................................... $19.99

MIX MASTERS
by Maureen Droney
50448023 Book..................................... $24.95

THE SINGER-SONGWRITER'S GUIDE TO RECORDING IN THE HOME STUDIO
by Shane Adams
00148211 Book/Online Audio............. $19.99

UNDERSTANDING AUDIO
by Daniel M. Thompson
50449456 Book..................................... $24.99

HAL•LEONARD® CORPORATION
7777 W. Bluemound Rd. P.O. Box 13819 Milwaukee, WI 53213

Prices subject to change without notice. Visit your local music dealer or bookstore, or go to **www.berkleepress.com**

SONGWRITING, COMPOSING, ARRANGING

ARRANGING FOR HORNS
by Jerry Gates
00121625 Book/Online Audio............ $19.99

ARRANGING FOR LARGE JAZZ ENSEMBLE
by Dick Lowell and Ken Pullig
50449528 Book/CD $39.95

BEGINNING SONGWRITING
by Andrea Stolpe with Jan Stolpe
00138503 Book/Online Audio $19.99

COMPLETE GUIDE TO FILM SCORING – 2ND ED.
by Richard Davis
50449607 .... $27.99

JAZZ COMPOSITION
by Ted Pease
50448000 Book/Online Audio $39.99

MELODY IN SONGWRITING
by Jack Perricone
50449419 Book/CD............................. $24.95

MODERN JAZZ VOICINGS
by Ted Pease and Ken Pullig
50449485 Book/CD............................. $24.95

MUSIC COMPOSITION FOR FILM AND TELEVISION
by Lalo Schifrin
50449604 Book $34.99

MUSIC NOTATION
PREPARING SCORES AND PARTS
by Matthew Nicholl and Richard Grudzinski
50449540 Book..................................... $16.99

MUSIC NOTATION
THEORY AND TECHNIQUE FOR MUSIC NOTATION
by Mark McGrain
50449399 Book..................................... $24.95

POPULAR LYRIC WRITING
by Andrea Stolpe
50449553 Book $14.95

SONGWRITING: ESSENTIAL GUIDE
Lyric and Form Structure
by Pat Pattison
50481582 Book..................................... $16.99
Rhyming
by Pat Pattison
00124366 2nd Ed. Book $17.99

SONGWRITING STRATEGIES
by Mark Simos
50449621 Book/CD.............................. $22.99

THE SONGWRITER'S WORKSHOP
Harmony
by Jimmy Kachulis
50449519 Book/Online Audio $29.95
Melody
by Jimmy Kachulis
50449518 Book/CD $24.95

AUTOBIOGRAPHY

LEARNING TO LISTEN: THE JAZZ JOURNEY OF GARY BURTON
by Gary Burton
00117798 Book $27.99